Celebrities and Journalists Say Goodbye to Musk's Social Platform

Jamie Lee Curtis, Don Lemon, and The Guardian Call It Quits Over Political and Legal Shifts

Lindsey T. Gordon

COPYRIGHT

TABLE OF CONTENTS

INTRODUCTION

The Rise and Fall of Twitter Under Elon Musk's Ownership

The transformation of Twitter into X under the ownership of Elon Musk represents one of the most significant shifts in the history of social media platforms. What began as a simple microblogging platform known for its brevity and real-time news updates has now evolved into something entirely different—a space increasingly marked by controversy, confusion, and heightened political engagement.

Musk's acquisition of Twitter in 2022 for a reported $44 billion set the stage for this transformation, but the consequences of his leadership have led to profound changes in the platform's culture, its legal landscape, and its role in shaping global conversations.

Upon Musk's purchase, many users, particularly celebrities and journalists, voiced concerns about what they perceived as a deterioration of Twitter's core values—free speech, transparency, and a space for open debate. As Musk's influence grew, so did the platform's shift toward more polarized, divisive content. For many, the departure of long-standing figures from the platform became a symbol of the widening chasm between the ideals that Twitter once represented and the direction Musk was steering it toward.

This book aims to explore the stories behind the public exits of notable figures such as

Jamie Lee Curtis, Don Lemon, and The Guardian, who decided to cut ties with X at a time when the platform was undergoing a major political and legal transformation. Their departures are not just personal decisions—they reflect broader societal and cultural shifts and raise critical questions about the role of social media in modern discourse.

As influential voices left the platform, they made statements that resonated far beyond their personal accounts. Their exits from X serve as a powerful commentary on the complex relationship between media, politics, and digital platforms in today's world.

Jamie Lee Curtis' Departure

Jamie Lee Curtis, an actress with a long-standing public profile, made headlines when she announced her departure from Twitter, shortly after its rebranding as X. Curtis, known for her outspoken views on various social issues, posted a simple yet poignant message on Instagram explaining her decision to deactivate her account.

In her message, she referenced the Serenity Prayer, a well-known invocation for peace and acceptance. Her departure highlighted a growing frustration among celebrities who once saw Twitter as a place for connection, but who now felt that the platform had become too toxic and polarized under Musk's leadership.

For Curtis, leaving X was not just about a disagreement with Musk's policies; it was a personal choice grounded in a desire for peace of mind and the pursuit of more positive, fulfilling engagements. Curtis' decision to leave the platform mirrored a larger trend of individuals and celebrities moving away from social media environments that no longer felt conducive to healthy discourse. Her deactivation of the account marked a broader disenchantment with social media's increasingly hostile nature.

Don Lemon's Exit and Legal Disputes

Similarly, Don Lemon, the former CNN anchor, became one of the most high-profile figures to publicly announce his departure from X. For Lemon, the platform's evolving landscape was no longer in line with his values, especially after Musk's acquisition. His relationship with X had been contentious for months prior to his decision to leave. Notably, Lemon had filed a lawsuit against Musk after a scrapped content partnership deal, and his exit from the platform came shortly after new terms of service were introduced, which directed all legal disputes to be settled in Texas.

In a heartfelt Instagram Reel, Lemon explained that he had once believed Twitter (now X) to be a space for honest debate and transparent discussion, a sentiment that mirrored the platform's original mission. However, Lemon expressed disappointment that X no longer served that purpose. He cited the platform's shift in focus and the introduction of terms that he found unfavorable as key reasons for his departure.

The platform's new legal framework, which effectively moved any disputes to the conservative-leaning courts of Texas, was a final straw for Lemon. He voiced concerns that this change would not only be disadvantageous to critics of Musk's policies but could also be used to shield the platform from legal repercussions, particularly in relation to its content moderation practices.

Lemon's exit, much like Curtis' departure, was emblematic of a broader trend in which those in the public eye—particularly journalists—felt compelled to leave X due to its evolving and increasingly politicized environment.

The Guardian's Departure and the Decline of Trust

The Guardian, a major UK-based newspaper with an international presence, also announced its decision to leave X. The outlet's decision was framed as a response to the growing toxicity on the platform, including the rise of far-right conspiracy theories, racism, and hate speech. The Guardian had long been critical of the changes Musk was implementing on the platform, but its official departure marked a significant moment in the ongoing debate about the role of social media in fostering healthy, responsible public discourse.

The Guardian's exit was a reflection of the deepening divide between progressive media outlets and X, whose political orientation under Musk's ownership was increasingly seen as out of touch with the values of many journalistic institutions.

The Guardian stated that it no longer believed the benefits of engaging with X outweighed the risks. The decision to withdraw was driven by the paper's commitment to promoting journalism and ensuring its integrity in an increasingly polarized media landscape. Furthermore, the outlet recognized that its business model—being directly funded by readers rather than dependent on social media algorithms—allowed it to make such a move without significant financial consequences.

This departure also highlighted the growing skepticism about X's ability to uphold journalistic standards, especially as Musk's own political affiliations seemed to align more closely with certain factions, raising concerns about the platform's neutrality.

A Broader Context of Departure

Curtis, Lemon, and The Guardian represent a broader shift in how celebrities, journalists, and media outlets view their engagement with social media platforms. What once served as a space for real-time updates, discussions, and networking has, under Musk's stewardship, turned into a politically charged environment, where speech and content moderation are highly contested.

The exodus of high-profile figures like Curtis and Lemon raises important questions: Has social media become too dangerous for meaningful discourse? Can platforms that prioritize free speech truly be balanced when commercial interests and political biases become intertwined?

As these public figures step away from X, their departures are not just personal decisions—they are a reflection of a much larger societal shift. Celebrities and journalists are increasingly seeking spaces that align more closely with their personal values and ethical standards, signaling a potential redefinition of how social media platforms should function in the modern world.

Through their stories, this book will explore how the actions of public figures—who once shaped Twitter's identity—reflect a broader dissatisfaction with a platform that, for many, has lost its way under new ownership.

The rise and fall of Twitter, now X, continues to unfold as its users confront these changes. The exit of public figures like Curtis, Lemon, and The Guardian suggests that Musk's vision for the platform may not be one that aligns with the values that initially made Twitter an integral part of global digital culture.

CHAPTER ONE

The Evolution of Twitter into X

The transformation of Twitter into X marks a pivotal moment in the history of social media platforms. Twitter, once a straightforward microblogging tool, became a global powerhouse of real-time news, conversations, and viral trends. However, under the leadership of Elon Musk, the platform began a dramatic and often controversial shift, evolving from a space of free-flowing information to a highly charged, polarized environment.

The transition from Twitter to X is a reflection of the larger changes Musk has imposed, affecting everything from the platform's ownership and leadership to its underlying culture and values. This chapter will explore the key moments that defined this transformation, beginning with Musk's acquisition of the platform and how his leadership has redefined its identity, followed by the cultural shifts that have shaped the platform's user experience.

The Acquisition by Elon Musk

In April 2022, Elon Musk made waves by offering to purchase Twitter for $44 billion. His initial proposal, which came as a surprise to many, was motivated by a desire to reform what he saw as a platform that had lost its way. Musk, known for his leadership of companies like Tesla and SpaceX, had been a vocal critic of Twitter's content moderation policies, which he argued stifled free speech and suppressed certain viewpoints.

His buyout of Twitter was, therefore, framed as an opportunity to restore the platform to its supposed original purpose: a space for open dialogue, transparency, and the exchange of ideas without the heavy hand of moderation or censorship.

The acquisition itself was a dramatic affair, fraught with legal battles, delays, and public drama. Musk initially proposed buying Twitter, but the deal soon became entangled in a series of complications. Musk raised concerns over the number of fake accounts on the platform, and at one point tried to back out of the deal. However, after months of legal wrangling, he ultimately completed the purchase in October 2022. Once in control, Musk immediately set about making sweeping changes to the platform's leadership, business model, and content policies.

Musk's acquisition was not just a corporate transaction—it was the start of a massive overhaul of Twitter's identity. Almost immediately, he moved to make drastic changes, including laying off a large percentage of Twitter's staff, introducing new subscription models, and eliminating features that had previously been fundamental to the platform's structure, such as verification protocols. Musk also made headlines by altering Twitter's long-standing policies around content moderation, pushing for fewer restrictions on what users could post, and sparking debates about the role of social media in moderating speech.

As Musk took the reins, he also made it clear that he viewed Twitter as a tool for shaping societal conversations, often voicing opinions on political issues and government regulation. His vision for the platform became less about enabling dialogue and more about creating a space where his ideals of free speech could flourish. This marked the beginning of what would later become X.

The Impact of Musk's Leadership

Musk's leadership had an immediate and far-reaching impact on Twitter's culture. Under his ownership, the platform became less a place for neutral discourse and more a reflection of his personal ideologies. The changes he made, particularly regarding content moderation and political influence, quickly became a point of contention among users, celebrities, journalists, and advertisers.

The first major change under Musk's leadership was the mass layoffs of Twitter's staff. Musk cut thousands of employees, citing the need to reduce costs and streamline operations. These layoffs raised questions about Twitter's ability to maintain its quality of service and effectively address issues like content moderation, harassment, and misinformation. The reduction in staff, particularly in the moderation and safety departments, led to an increase in harmful and inappropriate content on the platform.

Critics argued that Musk's "hands-off" approach to content moderation created an environment where misinformation, hate speech, and conspiracy theories thrived unchecked.

Musk's changes to Twitter's business model were equally significant. He introduced a subscription service, Twitter Blue, which offered users the ability to pay for verification, editing capabilities, and other features. This move was seen as an attempt to monetize the platform more aggressively, but it also led to concerns about the platform becoming increasingly pay-to-play, where the voices of regular users were drowned out by those with financial resources.

Another key aspect of Musk's leadership was his decision to reduce Twitter's reliance on advertisers and attempt to shift the platform's revenue model. This, too, caused friction with many of Twitter's longstanding corporate partners, who expressed concern about the platform's direction under Musk's ownership. Musk's combative approach to advertisers, coupled with his controversial statements about content moderation, led some to distance themselves from Twitter, further exacerbating the platform's financial instability.

Musk's leadership also brought heightened political tension to the platform. His public support for certain political candidates and ideologies sparked debates about the role of social media in influencing political discourse.

As he made decisions about the platform's policies, many began to question whether Twitter was becoming a tool for Musk's personal and political agenda. This was compounded by his decision to allow previously banned figures—such as former President Donald Trump—back onto the platform, a move that alienated many users and advertisers who were uncomfortable with the platform's newfound permissiveness toward controversial content.

Musk's approach to Twitter was one of disruption—he sought to break the platform's traditional structure in order to make it more aligned with his vision of free speech, even if it meant sacrificing the civility and safety that many users had come to expect. In doing so, Musk introduced a new level of volatility to the platform, changing how users interacted with Twitter and how they viewed its role in the broader social media ecosystem.

The Shift in Platform Culture and Values

As Twitter transformed into X, the cultural shift became even more pronounced. What had once been a space for real-time news, cultural commentary, and social engagement underpinned by a core set of community guidelines was now increasingly marked by a looser regulatory framework, a focus on individual expression, and a tolerance for controversial, even harmful content. This shift was not simply a change in the platform's operational structure—it was a radical transformation of its very identity.

At the heart of this cultural shift was Musk's redefinition of free speech. Under the old Twitter regime, the platform had a set of guidelines designed to curb misinformation, harassment, and hate speech. Musk's philosophy, however, was rooted in a more libertarian view of free speech, where the idea was that all ideas, no matter how controversial, should be allowed to circulate without restriction.

This hands-off approach to content moderation was met with strong reactions.

Some users welcomed the newfound freedom to express opinions that had previously been censored or flagged. Others, particularly those from marginalized communities, felt that the platform had become unsafe, and the absence of content moderation allowed hate speech, racism, and disinformation to spread unchecked.

The shift in platform culture was also evident in how the user base began to evolve. As Musk loosened restrictions, a greater influx of far-right voices, conspiracy theorists, and extremist groups began to dominate conversations on the platform. This shift created an environment where users who once felt that Twitter was a safe space for dialogue now found themselves at odds with others who felt emboldened to push extremist agendas. The platform became increasingly fragmented, as various factions clashed over the definition of free speech, with many users leaving or reducing their engagement.

Additionally, Musk's focus on monetizing Twitter through the introduction of features like Twitter Blue had a significant impact on the platform's culture. The idea of paying for features that were once free, such as verification and the ability to edit tweets, led to questions about accessibility and fairness. For many, this move represented the commercialization of a platform that had previously been a space for organic interaction and engagement. Instead of leveling the playing field, Musk's changes created a tiered system where those with the financial means to pay for premium features gained a significant advantage over those who could not.

As Twitter became X, the platform's cultural values became more aligned with Musk's personal philosophy, which emphasized individual expression over collective responsibility. This shift alienated many users who had valued the old Twitter's emphasis on dialogue and the ability to engage with diverse voices in a relatively civil manner.

The platform's new identity as X—with its less regulated environment and a focus on free expression—has led to a new era in social media, but one that raises important questions about the future of online communities, digital communication, and the role of social media in shaping public discourse.

Overall, the transition from Twitter to X under Elon Musk's leadership has been a tumultuous one, characterized by significant changes to the platform's culture, values, and overall mission. What was once a vibrant, if chaotic, space for global conversation has evolved into a more polarized and commercially driven environment. The impact of Musk's leadership has reshaped the platform in ways that will continue to influence the social media landscape for years to come.

CHAPTER TWO

Jamie Lee Curtis' Departure from X

In the ever-evolving world of social media, the departure of prominent figures can be as impactful as their arrival. Jamie Lee Curtis, the celebrated actress known for her roles in iconic films like "Halloween," made waves when she announced her decision to leave X (formerly Twitter) in November 2024. Curtis, whose career spans decades and whose social media presence is widely regarded as influential, is a prime example of the deepening disconnect between celebrities and the platforms they once championed.

Her decision to deactivate her X account marked not only a personal departure but also a broader commentary on the state of the platform under Elon Musk's leadership. This chapter explores the significance of Curtis' announcement, the symbolism behind her use of the Serenity Prayer, and the larger implications of celebrity influence on social media trends.

Curtis' Announcement and Social Media Influence

Jamie Lee Curtis' departure from X was far from a typical social media exit. Curtis, who had a long history of engaging with fans and followers on Twitter before Musk's acquisition, posted a screenshot of her account's deactivation alongside a message that resonated deeply with her audience. While other celebrities and journalists had been vocal about their frustrations with X's new direction, Curtis' post was not simply a farewell; it was a statement on the shifting landscape of social media and the personal decisions that stem from that shift.

By sharing her decision publicly on Instagram, Curtis tapped into the power of social media to amplify her message. While her departure from X may have seemed like a personal decision, it was a reflection of broader cultural trends regarding the platform's evolving nature.

Curtis had long been an advocate for using social media for good—connecting with fans, promoting causes, and even engaging in playful banter. But as X transformed under Musk's ownership, Curtis' relationship with the platform soured, particularly as concerns about misinformation, harassment, and the platform's increasingly polarized tone became more pronounced.

Curtis' influence on social media is undeniable. She boasts millions of followers on various platforms, and her posts often receive widespread attention, not only from her fanbase but also from media outlets and industry peers. She has long been seen as a voice of reason and positivity in the often toxic world of celebrity culture.

In her departure from X, Curtis joins a growing list of influential public figures—including Don Lemon and The Guardian—who have distanced themselves from Musk's controversial platform. This move serves as a signal to her audience, both as a personal decision and as a critique of a space that no longer aligns with her values.

As a veteran of the public eye, Curtis understands the power of influence. Her decision to leave X carries weight not only because of her fame but also because it underscores the growing trend of public figures evaluating the ethical implications of their digital platforms. Curtis' departure is emblematic of a larger cultural shift, where public figures are taking more care in curating their online presence, especially in the face of rapid shifts in platform culture and ownership.

The Serenity Prayer as a Reflection of Her Departure

One of the most poignant elements of Curtis' exit was her use of the Serenity Prayer in her announcement. The Serenity Prayer, often associated with the Twelve-Step recovery programs, is a well-known invocation that encourages wisdom, acceptance, and the courage to act. By quoting this prayer in her post, Curtis conveyed a sense of peace and resignation, signaling that her departure from X was not rooted in anger or frustration, but rather in a calm, reasoned understanding of the situation.

The Serenity Prayer reflects Curtis' personal philosophy in navigating the challenges of life, and in this context, it acts as a subtle yet powerful metaphor for her decision to leave the platform. Curtis' words resonated with a sense of self-awareness—recognizing that the changes occurring on X were beyond her control and acknowledging that it was time to step away from a space that no longer served her. This theme of "acceptance" speaks to the broader frustration that many users, especially those in the celebrity and media spheres, have felt as the platform transitioned from Twitter to X under Musk's ownership.

The inclusion of the Serenity Prayer also highlights the emotional toll that social media can take on individuals, particularly those in the public eye. Curtis has been vocal about the mental and emotional challenges that come with fame, especially in the age of social media, where every post and interaction is amplified. Her departure, framed through the lens of serenity and acceptance, suggests that leaving the platform was a conscious choice for her mental well-being—a choice that many others in her position may also be considering.

By invoking the Serenity Prayer, Curtis not only underscored the personal nature of her decision but also connected her departure to a universal theme of finding peace in difficult circumstances. It speaks to the broader sense of disillusionment that many users feel as they navigate the increasingly divisive and toxic environment on platforms like X. In this sense, Curtis' departure is a metaphor for the emotional and ethical reckoning that many celebrities, journalists, and everyday users are facing as they reassess their relationship with social media platforms under Musk's leadership.

The Impact of Celebrity Influence on Social Media Trends

Jamie Lee Curtis' exit from X is part of a larger trend where celebrities are using their social media platforms not just to promote themselves or engage with fans, but to make statements about the platforms themselves. Celebrities have long been powerful figures in shaping social media trends—whether through viral campaigns, sponsored posts, or personal messages. However, as the landscape of social media changes, so too does the role of celebrities in influencing these platforms' culture.

Curtis' decision to leave X is symbolic of a broader shift in how celebrities interact with social media. In the past, many celebrities used platforms like Twitter (and later X) to connect directly with their fans, share personal moments, and build public personas. However, as platforms like X became increasingly politicized and divisive, many celebrities began to re-evaluate their presence online. Curtis, in particular, was known for her positive and inclusive tone on Twitter, and her departure signals that she no longer finds the platform a space where she can promote those values.

The exit of high-profile celebrities like Curtis can have significant ripple effects on social media trends. Fans and followers often look to celebrities not just for entertainment but for guidance on the digital spaces they inhabit. Curtis' departure from X is a form of advocacy, subtly encouraging her followers to consider their own relationships with the platform. Her move could inspire others—both celebrities and everyday users—to think critically about the platforms they engage with and the values they uphold.

Moreover, Curtis' departure is part of a broader narrative where public figures are increasingly aligned with their personal ethics and values. In an era of cancel culture, growing distrust in tech companies, and heightened political divisions, more celebrities are aligning their personal choices with larger social movements. Curtis' exit from X is a clear example of a celebrity taking a stand, signaling that sometimes the best way to influence change is by stepping away from a space that no longer serves their principles.

In this way, Curtis' decision contributes to the evolving dynamic between celebrities and social media platforms. As public figures become more discerning in how they use these platforms, their choices—whether to remain, speak out, or leave—can shape the conversation and influence the behavior of millions of followers. By stepping away from X, Curtis not only makes a statement about her own values but also encourages a larger dialogue about the role of social media in our lives and the influence it wields over our collective behavior.

Overall, Jamie Lee Curtis' departure from X underscores the power that celebrities hold in shaping social media trends and the growing importance of ethical considerations in the digital age. Her decision to step away, framed through the Serenity Prayer, highlights her personal quest for peace and alignment with her values, a sentiment that resonates deeply with many social media users.

In an era of increased polarization, Curtis' exit serves as a poignant reminder that even the most influential public figures must carefully consider the platforms they engage with and the impact those platforms have on their personal and professional identities.

CHAPTER THREE

Don Lemon's Exit and His Legal Battle

Don Lemon, the prominent journalist and former CNN anchor, made headlines when he announced his departure from X (formerly Twitter) in November 2024, joining a growing list of celebrities, journalists, and media outlets distancing themselves from the platform under Elon Musk's ownership. Lemon's decision was not simply the result of a personal preference, but rather an accumulation of frustration over the platform's evolving political and legal landscape.

His legal battles with Musk and X, combined with concerns about the ethical direction of the platform, made his exit a significant moment in the ongoing discourse about the future of social media. This chapter explores Lemon's long-standing relationship with Twitter, the legal confrontation that escalated tensions with Musk, and the ethical considerations that led him to sever ties with X.

Lemon's Long-Standing Connection to Twitter

Don Lemon's relationship with Twitter predates Musk's acquisition of the platform, making his departure all the more impactful. Lemon, known for his candid and often unfiltered commentary on social and political issues, had been an active and influential presence on Twitter for years. His account was a space for political commentary, personal insights, and interactions with his audience, especially during significant national events such as elections, social justice movements, and global crises. As a journalist, Twitter had served as a vital tool for him to communicate directly with the public, engage in debates, and share breaking news updates.

Lemon's use of Twitter was emblematic of the broader role that social media has come to play in modern journalism. For journalists like Lemon, Twitter was more than just a platform for self-promotion; it was an essential tool for professional communication, shaping public discourse, and providing real-time updates to millions of followers. The immediacy of Twitter allowed Lemon to engage with breaking news and offer his perspectives in a space that was increasingly becoming the epicenter of public debate.

However, as the platform transitioned into X under Elon Musk's leadership, many long-time users, including Lemon, began to feel the platform was no longer serving its original purpose. Musk's changes to Twitter—such as the introduction of new content moderation policies, the relaxation of hate speech rules, and the proliferation of misinformation—made the platform increasingly difficult to navigate, particularly for those in the media industry who relied on Twitter as a tool for journalistic integrity.

For Lemon, the shift in Twitter's identity was not merely a nuisance, but a fundamental betrayal of the platform's role in fostering transparency and open dialogue. Over time, his once positive experience with Twitter began to sour, culminating in his announcement to leave. This decision reflected not only his personal frustration with Musk's leadership but also the broader ethical concerns that many journalists, celebrities, and users were beginning to voice.

The Lawsuit Against Musk and X's Controversial Terms

Don Lemon's legal battle with Musk and X added another layer of complexity to his departure. In August 2024, Lemon filed a lawsuit against Musk over a scrapped content partnership deal with X. The lawsuit became a public flashpoint in the ongoing tension between Musk and key figures in the media. Lemon alleged that X had violated their agreement, leaving him in a vulnerable position professionally. This legal confrontation highlighted the growing friction between Musk's business practices and the media industry, particularly regarding content creation, partnerships, and editorial freedom.

The lawsuit against Musk was more than a contractual dispute; it was a reflection of the changing power dynamics within the digital media ecosystem. Musk's control over X had altered the way content was moderated, and his leadership had created a more adversarial environment for journalists and media figures. As the lawsuit unfolded, it became clear that Lemon's departure from the platform was not just a reaction to the changing culture on X but also a response to what he perceived as an unfair business practice.

Simultaneously, X's new terms of service, which went into effect in November 2024, became a central issue for Lemon. These terms outlined that all legal disputes would be brought exclusively in the U.S. District Court for the Northern District of Texas or in state courts located in Tarrant County, Texas. This was seen by many, including Lemon, as a tactic to limit the platform's exposure to litigation from critics. Lemon, who had already expressed concerns over X's political leanings and its effect on public discourse, viewed these legal changes as part of a broader pattern of protecting Musk's interests at the expense of transparency and fairness.

Lemon pointed out that by funneling legal disputes to a conservative hub like Texas, X was positioning itself to be more insulated from challenges, particularly those related to content moderation and free speech. The choice of venue for legal disputes seemed, to Lemon, like a deliberate move to shield X from litigation and suppress dissent. He saw it as an extension of the platform's increasingly partisan nature, one that marginalized critical voices and made it harder for users—especially journalists and media organizations—to challenge the platform's practices.

This combination of legal action, the controversial new terms, and the growing sense of disillusionment with Musk's management created the perfect storm for Lemon's decision to leave. The legal and business aspects of Lemon's departure were not just about one man's grievances with a tech giant; they reflected a larger trend in the media industry, where platforms like X were coming under scrutiny for their power to shape public discourse, stifle critical voices, and control the flow of information.

The Ethical Concerns Behind Lemon's Decision to Leave

Beyond the legal and business disputes, Don Lemon's decision to leave X was also rooted in deeper ethical concerns about the platform's direction under Musk's leadership. Lemon, a journalist with a long-standing reputation for tackling complex political and social issues, was deeply troubled by the increasing polarization of discourse on X. Under Musk, the platform had shifted in ways that many users, particularly journalists and media professionals, felt were damaging to the integrity of public dialogue.

One of Lemon's primary concerns was the platform's handling of misinformation and hate speech. As Musk loosened content moderation policies and allowed previously banned accounts to return, the platform became a breeding ground for conspiracy theories, harassment, and extremist content. For Lemon, whose career had been built on transparency and responsible journalism, these changes undermined the very principles that made platforms like Twitter important to public life. The platform was no longer a space for honest debate or responsible discussion, but rather a venue for political warfare and unchecked disinformation.

Lemon also expressed concern about the platform's growing partisanship. The relaxed content moderation policies, the prioritization of sensational content, and Musk's own outspoken political views created an environment that Lemon felt was increasingly hostile to journalists and media outlets that did not align with Musk's political leanings. Lemon's decision to leave X was not just a personal one; it was an ethical stand against a platform that, in his view, was no longer serving the public interest in the same way it once had.

Furthermore, the new legal framework that required all disputes to be handled in Texas raised additional ethical concerns. Lemon and other critics viewed this as an attempt to shield the platform from scrutiny and reduce its accountability for its role in spreading harmful content. For Lemon, the decision to leave X was an ethical one—he could no longer participate in a space that, in his opinion, no longer upheld the values of free speech, transparency, and responsible journalism.

In making his decision public, Lemon was not just distancing himself from a platform; he was sending a message to his audience and the media industry at large. His departure reflected the broader moral reckoning that many public figures and journalists were facing as they contended with the changing nature of social media under Musk's leadership. For Lemon, stepping away from X was not simply an act of personal frustration but a commitment to upholding the ethical standards he had long espoused in his career.

Overall, Don Lemon's exit from X was a culmination of legal, ethical, and personal considerations. His long-standing connection to Twitter, the legal battle with Musk, and the growing concerns about X's direction all played a significant role in his decision. Lemon's departure underscores the larger issue of how social media platforms are shaping public discourse, with figures like Lemon using their exits to make bold statements about the platforms' ethical responsibility.

As the digital media landscape continues to evolve, Lemon's decision is likely to inspire other journalists and public figures to reconsider their relationship with platforms like X, where the lines between free speech, partisanship, and corporate control are becoming increasingly blurred.

CHAPTER FOUR

The Guardian's Withdrawal from X

The Guardian, a major UK-based newspaper known for its global reach and commitment to quality journalism, made headlines in November 2024 with its decision to cease sharing content on X (formerly Twitter). This marked a significant shift for the media outlet, which had used the platform for years to distribute news, engage with readers, and build its audience. The Guardian's withdrawal from X was not simply a strategic business decision but a response to the evolving political, ethical, and financial landscape of social media platforms under Elon Musk's ownership.

This chapter delves into the reasons behind The Guardian's exit, exploring its criticisms of X's increasingly toxic environment, the changing role of journalism in the age of social media, and the financial implications for media outlets in an era where platforms like X play an outsized role in shaping public discourse.

The Paper's Criticism of X's Toxic Environment

The Guardian's decision to stop sharing content on X was primarily driven by its growing concerns about the platform's toxic environment. The paper released a statement that explicitly highlighted how the benefits of being on X had become outweighed by the increasingly negative aspects of the platform. One of the primary criticisms was the proliferation of harmful content, including far-right conspiracy theories, hate speech, and racism. For The Guardian, these toxic elements were not only a distraction but a threat to the integrity of the platform as a space for quality discourse.

The Guardian's editorial board had been monitoring the shifts in X's policies and practices under Elon Musk for months, and it became clear that the platform was veering into dangerous territory. As Musk loosened content moderation rules and allowed the return of controversial figures previously banned for spreading misinformation or engaging in hate speech, The Guardian found that X was increasingly unable to provide the space for responsible journalism it had once hoped for. The presence of extremist content and the normalization of hate speech on the platform made it an uncomfortable space for media outlets like The Guardian, which pride themselves on presenting fact-based, fair, and thoughtful analysis.

This shift was particularly problematic for The Guardian given its global reach and reputation as a progressive news source. The platform, once seen as a useful tool for sharing content with a broad audience, was now being viewed as an active enabler of political polarization. In a media environment where fact-checking and responsible reporting are more crucial than ever, X's policies under Musk were seen as counterproductive to these values. For The

Guardian, continuing to engage with a platform that was facilitating the spread of dangerous rhetoric no longer aligned with its journalistic mission.

The Guardian's criticism was not limited to X's content moderation practices; it also extended to Musk's political influence and the way his ownership of the platform was shaping discourse. As the social media landscape became more aligned with Musk's personal political views, The Guardian felt that the platform was moving away from its initial role as a space for diverse opinions and toward a more partisan, polarized environment.

This shift made it harder for The Guardian to maintain its journalistic independence and integrity on a platform that was increasingly becoming a tool for political maneuvering rather than an open forum for public debate.

The Role of Journalism in the Era of Social Media

The Guardian's departure from X is a reflection of the broader challenges facing journalism in the digital age, especially as social media platforms have become dominant in shaping public discourse. The rise of platforms like Twitter—now X—has radically transformed the way news is consumed, distributed, and discussed. For news organizations, social media has provided a direct channel to reach readers, expand their audience, and engage in real-time reporting. However, as these platforms have evolved, their relationship with traditional journalism has become increasingly fraught with tension.

In the era of social media, journalists and news outlets have had to adapt to a new reality where the speed of information dissemination and the scale of audience reach are paramount. Social media platforms are no longer just venues for news sharing but are central to the economic model of many media outlets. With millions of users engaging with content on a daily basis, platforms like X have become essential for drawing traffic to news websites, promoting stories, and generating revenue through advertising and user engagement.

However, as The Guardian's decision illustrates, the relationship between journalism and social media platforms is becoming more complicated. For reputable news organizations, the value of engaging with social media has to be balanced against the risks of amplifying misinformation, political extremism, and harmful content.

The role of journalists on platforms like X is increasingly seen as one of gatekeeping—ensuring that credible, fact-based reporting is not drowned out by noise, disinformation, and hate. But as the platform evolves, this task becomes increasingly difficult. The ethical responsibility of journalists to maintain their credibility and independence has led many to question whether engaging with a platform like X is still tenable.

For The Guardian, this dilemma became untenable as X's direction diverged more sharply from the values it held as a media outlet. By continuing to use X as a distribution platform, The Guardian would have been complicit in a system that allowed harmful content to flourish and weakened the public's trust in responsible journalism.

As a result, The Guardian decided to sever its ties with the platform, marking a critical turning point in the relationship between journalism and social media. This decision speaks to the larger issue of how media outlets must navigate the complexities of social media's influence on journalism in an era where platforms are both essential for reach and fraught with ethical risks.

The Financial Implications for Media Outlets on Social Platforms

The Guardian's withdrawal from X also carries significant financial implications, particularly for media outlets that have built their business models around social media engagement. In the early days of Twitter (now X), news outlets, blogs, and digital publications embraced the platform as a tool for driving traffic, increasing readership, and generating advertising revenue. With millions of users posting and engaging with content every day, social media platforms offered media organizations a direct route to their audience, bypassing traditional distribution methods like print media.

For many news outlets, including The Guardian, this integration of social media into their business strategies became essential for survival in an increasingly digital world. As traditional revenue streams like print advertising waned, the traffic driven by social media platforms became a lifeline. The Guardian had relied on its large following on X to promote stories, engage with readers, and increase website visits. As the platform grew, so did the potential for monetizing content through ads and sponsored posts, making social media engagement a key part of the paper's financial strategy.

However, as the platform's tone shifted under Musk's leadership and its focus moved away from news and more toward entertainment and partisan content, the financial value of being on X became less clear. For The Guardian, the cost of maintaining a presence on a platform where the audience was increasingly drawn to sensationalist content, conspiracy theories, and extreme political discourse outweighed the potential benefits. Additionally, the toxicity of the platform and the growing concerns about disinformation meant that The Guardian could no longer engage with X without risking its own credibility and reputation.

The financial implications of The Guardian's withdrawal are significant, as it signals a potential shift in the way media outlets approach social media engagement. As X's future remains uncertain and other platforms like Meta's Facebook and Instagram continue to dominate, media outlets may need to rethink their strategies for digital engagement. The Guardian's decision suggests that, in some cases, the long-term financial benefits of social media may no longer justify the ethical and reputational risks associated with staying on platforms that have evolved in ways that run counter to journalistic integrity.

The Guardian's exit also raises broader questions about the sustainability of social media as a revenue model for news outlets. If more publications begin to follow suit and withdraw from platforms like X, it could signal a paradigm shift in the way digital media works, forcing platforms to rethink how they monetize content and how they manage relationships with media organizations.

This could have far-reaching implications for the future of online journalism, as news outlets may have to invest in more sustainable, independent methods of reaching their audiences without relying on social media platforms that are increasingly prone to controversy and criticism.

Overall, the Guardian's withdrawal from X is a significant moment in the evolution of social media's role in journalism. It reflects the deepening ethical, political, and financial challenges that media outlets face as they navigate an increasingly polarized and toxic social media landscape.

As X and other platforms continue to evolve, the decisions made by institutions like The Guardian will shape the future of online journalism and influence the ways in which news is disseminated, consumed, and monetized in the digital age.

CHAPTER FIVE

The Changing Role of Free Speech on X

The concept of free speech has been at the center of the debate surrounding Elon Musk's takeover of X (formerly Twitter). As one of Musk's central claims throughout his acquisition of the platform was the commitment to making X a bastion of free speech, the reality of his actions has led to growing controversy and increasing concern from both public figures and media outlets.

This chapter explores how Musk's approach to free speech and content moderation has altered the platform's landscape, the rise of far-right conspiracy theories and misinformation under his leadership, and the evolving meaning of free speech for public figures, journalists, and ordinary users of the platform.

Musk's Approach to Free Speech and Content Moderation

When Elon Musk took control of Twitter in 2022, one of his primary promises was to make the platform a more open forum for free speech. He emphasized his belief that Twitter had previously been overly restrictive in its content moderation, with certain political and ideological voices being silenced under the guise of protecting users from harmful content.

Musk's stated goal was to transform the platform into a place where diverse opinions could be heard, even if they were controversial or offensive. He advocated for minimal intervention, allowing users more freedom to express themselves without fear of censorship.

Upon taking ownership of Twitter, Musk quickly set about dismantling much of the platform's previous content moderation framework. High-profile bans were lifted, including those of controversial figures like former U.S. President Donald Trump, conspiracy theorists, and other individuals who had been banned for spreading hate speech, misinformation, and inciting violence.

Musk's supporters argued that this marked the return of true free speech—where all voices, regardless of their content, could be heard without fear of suppression. This approach, Musk claimed, would better reflect a more open, democratic society, with users acting as the arbiters of what should be acceptable.

However, critics of Musk's approach contend that by reducing content moderation, X became a breeding ground for harmful rhetoric and dangerous content. The platform's decision to allow more unregulated speech gave rise to an environment where hate speech, misinformation, and harassment flourished. For many users and former supporters of the platform, this shift led to a sense of uncertainty about whether free speech, as Musk envisioned it, could coexist with the protection of vulnerable communities, truth, and safety on the platform.

Musk's definition of free speech appears to prioritize the rights of individuals to express their opinions, even when those opinions are harmful or factually incorrect. This has led to a series of contradictions in how X handles controversial topics. While Musk continues to champion the idea that the platform should allow "unfiltered" discourse, critics argue that the platform has become a haven for those seeking to spread division, racism, and disinformation.

The growing presence of extreme voices on the platform has prompted questions about whether Musk's commitment to free speech is being used as a cover for enabling toxic behavior, rather than fostering genuine, constructive debate.

This complex balancing act—between promoting freedom of expression and maintaining a safe, respectful space for users—has made Musk's leadership on X increasingly contentious. The changing role of free speech under his direction highlights the challenges social media platforms face in determining where to draw the line between protecting individual rights and ensuring that the platform does not become a tool for abuse, hate, and misinformation.

The Growing Influence of Far-Right Conspiracy Theories

One of the most significant consequences of Musk's approach to free speech has been the rise of far-right conspiracy theories and extremist content on X. By reducing moderation efforts and allowing previously banned figures back onto the platform, X has become a magnet for extremist voices, many of whom espouse dangerous ideologies, conspiracy theories, and hate speech. This shift has led to an increase in the visibility of far-right movements, which often use social media platforms to organize, spread their messages, and recruit new followers.

Among the most notable conspiracy theories that have gained traction on X since Musk's takeover are those related to QAnon, anti-vaccine rhetoric, and election denialism. Musk's decision to reinstate accounts associated with these movements has allowed them to regain a significant foothold on the platform. As a result, the spread of misinformation has become a major concern for both users and media outlets, which now have to contend with the fact that far-right groups are using X to manipulate public opinion, spread lies, and foment division.

Musk's relaxed stance on content moderation has given conspiracy theorists a platform to amplify their voices and reach wider audiences. The proliferation of QAnon posts and anti-science narratives has led many to question whether Musk's commitment to free speech is empowering individuals and groups that threaten the public good.

This shift in the platform's dynamics has prompted a growing backlash from concerned users, public figures, and advocacy organizations, who argue that the presence of far-right conspiracy theories on X is not only dangerous but also undermines the credibility of the platform itself.

Furthermore, the influence of these conspiracy theories has spilled over into real-world events, with many online movements using X to organize protests, spread fake news, and even incite violence. The rise of disinformation campaigns and coordinated harassment campaigns against political opponents, journalists, and minority groups has made X a volatile space, especially in the lead-up to major political events such as elections.

The increased visibility of extremist voices on the platform has resulted in a public relations crisis for Musk, as he grapples with the consequences of his free speech absolutism in a world where harmful ideas can spread at an unprecedented scale.

While Musk argues that these movements should be allowed to voice their opinions on the platform, critics assert that by permitting such content, he is enabling dangerous groups to shape the political discourse in a way that undermines democratic principles and social cohesion. The growing influence of far-right conspiracy theories on X is one of the most contentious issues facing the platform and represents a major challenge to Musk's vision of free speech.

What Free Speech Means for Public Figures and Journalists

For public figures, including politicians, celebrities, and journalists, the evolving concept of free speech on X has significant implications. As social media platforms become central to how public figures communicate with their audiences, they must contend with the balance between expressing their opinions freely and protecting themselves from harassment, misinformation, and threats.

Journalists, in particular, face unique challenges when it comes to free speech on platforms like X. Social media has become a primary tool for journalists to engage with the public, share breaking news, and promote their reporting. However, with the decline in content moderation, many journalists have found themselves the targets of coordinated harassment campaigns, disinformation attacks, and even threats of violence. The lack of robust protection against harmful content on X has raised concerns about the safety and integrity of journalists who rely on the platform to communicate with their audiences.

For public figures and journalists, free speech on X has become a double-edged sword. While Musk's commitment to allowing unfettered expression on the platform gives users the right to engage in open debate, it also exposes them to risks, including online abuse, harassment, and reputational damage. The chaotic nature of discourse on X, where misinformation and extremist content flourish, makes it difficult for public figures to maintain a healthy relationship with the platform without sacrificing their personal safety or the credibility of their work.

Moreover, the decision to remain on X has increasingly become a political statement in itself. For journalists, the question of whether to engage with the platform is no longer solely about reaching an audience but also about aligning with a platform that has become synonymous with divisive and controversial content. This has forced public figures to make tough decisions about whether to participate in a platform that could expose them to attack or risk alienating their audiences by leaving it altogether.

In essence, free speech on X has come to mean different things for different groups. For Musk and his supporters, it represents the triumph of individual expression without limits. For many public figures and journalists, however, it has come to signify a battleground where their right to speak freely is increasingly threatened by the toxic and dangerous environment fostered by Musk's leadership. As X continues to evolve, the meaning of free speech will remain a critical point of contention, with profound implications for the future of discourse on social media and its role in public life.

Overall, this chapter explores how Musk's vision of free speech has altered the dynamics of X, turning it into a more controversial and polarized platform. As public figures and journalists continue to wrestle with the implications of Musk's leadership and the growing influence of extremist content, the future of free speech on X remains uncertain.

The changing nature of discourse on the platform poses critical questions about the balance between openness and responsibility in the digital age, especially as it pertains to those who use the platform to shape public opinion and drive societal change.

CHAPTER SIX

Political Influence and Its Impact on Social Media

The intersection of politics and social media has always been a critical concern, but with Elon Musk's acquisition of Twitter, now X, this dynamic has taken on a new intensity. Musk's political involvement, particularly his close ties with former President Donald Trump and his outspoken political views, has led many to question how these affiliations shape the direction of X and its role in shaping political discourse. As Musk's political leanings and involvement become more apparent, the platform is increasingly seen as a vehicle for political influence, with ramifications for both the users of X and the broader landscape of social media.

This chapter delves into Musk's political involvement and its profound effect on X, particularly as it relates to his appointment within Trump's administration, and the broader consequences of political shifts for public trust in social platforms.

Elon Musk's Political Involvement and Its Effect on X

Since taking ownership of Twitter in 2022, Elon Musk has made it clear that his political views shape his decisions as the platform's owner. Musk, known for his libertarian leanings, has been vocal about his beliefs in free speech and limited government intervention, positioning himself as an advocate for open, unregulated discourse. However, his increasingly visible political involvement—especially his public support for right-wing causes—has raised eyebrows among users, critics, and politicians alike.

Musk's political involvement is particularly evident in his support for former President Donald Trump and his participation in various political events. Musk's backing of Trump, both financially and in public statements, has brought him into close alignment with conservative political ideologies.

Musk's ownership of X has led to suspicions that the platform may be used as a tool to push a certain political agenda, especially as he has reinstated controversial figures banned for spreading misinformation, hate speech, and violent rhetoric. Critics argue that Musk's ownership of X has allowed for the further promotion of far-right political ideologies, conspiracy theories, and misinformation.

Musk's political contributions, as well as his public comments about political issues, have made it increasingly difficult to separate his political identity from the platform he oversees. While Musk has claimed that his goal is to restore free speech, his critics see his actions as favoring specific political narratives and groups. The presence of far-right extremists, the reinstatement of former President Trump's account, and the diminishing of content moderation all point to a political influence that's steering the direction of X in ways that many users find concerning.

As a result, the platform has become more polarized, with many users questioning whether it can remain a neutral space for public discourse. Musk's political involvement, and his ability to shape the platform's policies, raise concerns about X's role as a propaganda tool and whether its neutrality can be maintained in an increasingly politicized climate.

Trump's Appointment of Musk to the Administration

In late 2024, President Donald Trump announced that he had appointed Elon Musk to a prominent position within his administration—a move that has amplified concerns about the intertwining of politics and social media. Musk's new role, as co-head of the so-called Department of Government Efficiency, which aims to overhaul federal bureaucracy and reduce regulations, marks a clear endorsement of Musk by Trump, and it positions the tech mogul as a key player in shaping political discourse in America.

This appointment has raised serious questions about the relationship between Musk's political influence and his ownership of X. Critics argue that Musk's involvement in government while overseeing a major social media platform presents a potential conflict of interest. As the owner of X, Musk holds significant sway over the platform's policies, algorithms, and content moderation practices, and now, as part of Trump's administration, he is in a position to influence government decisions that could directly impact the platform's operations.

Musk's role in Trump's administration also has implications for how X will be used in the 2024 U.S. presidential election. With Trump's account reinstated and Musk publicly supportive of the former president, it's clear that X could play a central role in the election, especially in terms of shaping the public's perception of candidates and political events. Musk's leadership of X, combined with his political influence, raises questions about whether the platform will serve as a neutral forum for debate or whether it will become a political battleground that serves the interests of certain political factions.

The decision to appoint Musk—an outspoken advocate for deregulation and a vocal supporter of Trump—raises further concerns about the role of social media platforms in shaping political outcomes. Will X be used to push specific political agendas, amplify partisan voices, and control the narrative around key issues? Musk's dual role as a tech mogul and a political influencer raises alarms about the potential for media manipulation and the erosion of public trust in the platform's ability to offer objective, unbiased information.

How Political Shifts Affect Public Trust in Social Platforms

The political shifts occurring at the intersection of Musk's leadership of X and his involvement with Trump's administration have profound consequences for public trust in the platform and social media in general. Social media has long been seen as a powerful tool for political discourse, activism, and information-sharing, but with the increasing politicization of platforms like X, many users are questioning whether these spaces can remain objective, impartial, and trustworthy.

Public trust in social media platforms is deeply intertwined with perceptions of neutrality and transparency. When users feel that a platform is being used to promote a particular political agenda or ideology, their confidence in the integrity of the platform begins to erode. Musk's openly partisan behavior and his support for far-right political causes have created a climate of distrust on X, particularly among users who feel that the platform's content moderation policies are being swayed by political interests.

The changing political landscape under Musk's leadership is also contributing to a sense of polarization on X. Many users report feeling increasingly isolated, as the platform becomes more divided along political lines. As the platform amplifies partisan content, it becomes harder for users to engage in meaningful, respectful debate.

This shift is especially concerning for journalists, who rely on platforms like X to connect with audiences and share important news. The erosion of public trust in X has made many question whether the platform can still be relied upon as a source of factual information or if it has become a political echo chamber.

Moreover, the broader trend of political interference in social media platforms has had implications beyond X. Other platforms, such as Facebook and Instagram, have faced similar criticisms regarding their role in political campaigns, misinformation, and electoral manipulation. As the influence of tech moguls like Musk grows, it raises the question of whether social media companies should be more heavily regulated to ensure that they are serving the public good rather than political or corporate interests.

The erosion of trust in X is also reflective of a broader trend in society, where political polarization is seeping into every aspect of public life, including social media. As political figures increasingly use social media to shape public opinion, it becomes harder for users to trust that the platforms are being used for genuine discourse and information-sharing rather than for political manipulation.

Public figures, journalists, and everyday users who once relied on platforms like X to engage in open, democratic debate are now grappling with the realization that their interactions may be influenced by political motives. For many, this realization signals a loss of faith in the power of social media to foster civil discourse and serve as a tool for positive political change.

Overall, this chapter highlights how the increasing political influence of Elon Musk, particularly through his involvement in Trump's administration, has affected X and the broader social media ecosystem. As Musk's political ties become more prominent, users are questioning the integrity of the platform and its ability to provide a neutral space for political discussion.

The growing politicization of social media platforms raises important questions about public trust, the role of tech moguls in shaping political discourse, and the future of free speech in digital spaces. As social media becomes more entwined with politics, its ability to serve the public good without being influenced by partisan interests is increasingly in doubt.

CHAPTER SEVEN

The New Terms of Service and Their Repercussions

The new terms of service that X (formerly Twitter) introduced in late 2024 marked a significant shift in how the platform conducts its legal and business affairs. The most notable change was the decision to require all legal disputes to be resolved exclusively in the U.S. District Court for the Northern District of Texas, or in state courts located in Tarrant County, Texas.

This move sparked widespread controversy, particularly among critics who viewed it as a strategy to benefit the platform and its owner, Elon Musk, politically and financially. These changes have far-reaching consequences not only for users but also for the broader conversation about corporate governance, legal accountability, and the role of social media in public discourse.

This chapter examines the ramifications of these new terms of service, focusing on the controversial decision to shift legal disputes to Texas, the potential biases that could result from this decision, and the broader corporate strategies that influence these decisions.

The Controversial Legal Shift to Texas Courts

The most controversial aspect of X's updated terms of service was the stipulation that any legal disputes with the platform must be brought before courts in Texas, specifically the U.S. District Court for the Northern District of Texas or state courts in Tarrant County. This decision has drawn significant criticism, particularly from users and legal experts who argue that it creates an unfair advantage for the platform and may have political undertones.

The rationale behind this shift is largely related to Musk's desire to minimize the legal risks associated with running a social media platform, especially one as influential and politically charged as X. Texas, home to Musk's companies SpaceX and Tesla, has long been seen as a favorable legal environment for business. The state has a reputation for being business-friendly and conservative in its legal and regulatory policies, which may have influenced Musk's decision to center legal disputes in Texas courts.

However, critics contend that this legal shift could lead to a significant power imbalance. By mandating that legal disputes be settled in Texas, Musk effectively limits the venues in which users can pursue legal action. This could deter individuals or organizations from suing the platform, especially if they are from outside the state or country. The change also raises questions about whether users' grievances can be heard impartially, given that Texas courts are perceived as being more sympathetic to conservative political viewpoints, aligning with Musk's own political leanings.

The decision has prompted fears that users who want to challenge the platform's policies, including issues related to free speech, content moderation, and censorship, may be unfairly disadvantaged by the shift in jurisdiction. The platform's new legal strategy seems to ensure that cases against X are more likely to be heard in a state with a legal environment that may favor Musk's position, which raises significant questions about fairness and the platform's commitment to accountability.

For users, the shift to Texas courts represents not only a logistical burden but also an erosion of access to justice. Many individuals who may be impacted by the platform's decisions are located far from Texas, and the financial and time commitments of pursuing a case in a distant jurisdiction could discourage them from holding the company accountable for its actions.

The Concerns Over Jurisdiction and Bias

Jurisdiction plays a crucial role in legal proceedings, as it determines which court has the authority to hear a case and which laws apply. The decision to mandate legal disputes in Texas courts raises concerns about potential biases and conflicts of interest, especially given Musk's ties to the state and its political climate.

Texas is known for its conservative legal environment, with judges often being appointed or elected based on their political affiliations. For Musk, who is an outspoken supporter of conservative causes and has forged close ties with conservative political figures, this legal shift could provide an advantageous forum for resolving disputes. Legal experts have noted that Texas courts may be less likely to rule in favor of plaintiffs who challenge the platform's content moderation policies, particularly in cases where the issues at hand involve free speech, discrimination, or censorship.

The choice of Texas as a jurisdictional hub for X's legal disputes suggests a strategic decision to align the platform's legal interests with the state's political and legal culture. Musk's political influence in the state—coupled with the platform's increasingly right-leaning policies—has led to concerns that the new terms of service could create a system where legal outcomes are not based solely on the facts of the case but are instead shaped by political factors.

Additionally, critics argue that this shift in jurisdiction could result in biased rulings that favor the interests of X, rather than offering fair treatment to users and plaintiffs. In a legal environment where conservative political ideologies are strongly represented, plaintiffs who challenge X's practices may be forced to confront legal obstacles that could undermine their chances of success.

Furthermore, the decision to require legal disputes to be heard in Texas could create a chilling effect on users and organizations who might otherwise seek redress for harms caused by the platform. Fear of an uphill legal battle in a jurisdiction that may be less sympathetic to their concerns could deter potential plaintiffs from pursuing cases altogether.

How Terms of Service Reflect Broader Corporate Strategies

The changes to X's terms of service are not just about legal maneuvering; they also reflect broader corporate strategies that prioritize business interests and control over user rights. By shifting legal disputes to Texas, X effectively strengthens its position in the face of growing scrutiny and criticism. These legal changes allow Musk and his team to minimize potential liabilities while simultaneously creating a more favorable environment for defending the platform against lawsuits.

The move also reflects Musk's broader approach to corporate governance. Musk has consistently promoted a vision of tech companies that are free from government interference and regulation, advocating for greater autonomy in how these platforms operate. By consolidating legal power in Texas, Musk can ensure that X remains insulated from external pressures, particularly from liberal states or progressive legal institutions that may challenge the platform's policies.

Additionally, the updated terms of service highlight how social media platforms are increasingly adopting corporate strategies that prioritize profits, power, and control over user experience and legal accountability. By enforcing these new terms, X signals that it is willing to prioritize corporate interests—whether through minimizing the financial impact of legal disputes or protecting its reputation from the negative consequences of high-profile lawsuits. This approach reflects a growing trend among tech giants to centralize power and limit user recourse, especially in the face of mounting legal and regulatory challenges.

These shifts in corporate strategy are part of a broader movement within the tech industry to tighten control over user data, content, and interactions, particularly as platforms become more entangled in political and ideological conflicts. By reshaping its terms of service to benefit from a more favorable legal environment, X is reinforcing the power dynamics that exist between tech companies and their users.

Moreover, the changes to X's terms of service can be seen as part of a wider trend in which companies, particularly in the tech sector, are pushing for greater corporate freedom in the face of growing public and governmental scrutiny. By shifting jurisdictional power and controlling legal outcomes, X is signaling that it intends to maintain a level of operational flexibility that allows it to pursue its business interests without being hindered by external forces.

Overall, this chapter illustrates how the changes to X's terms of service, particularly the shift to Texas courts, have sparked significant debate and concern among users, legal experts, and advocacy groups. The decision to move legal disputes to Texas reflects Musk's broader corporate strategies of consolidating power, minimizing liabilities, and controlling the narrative around the platform.

The implications of these changes extend beyond legal logistics, raising fundamental questions about fairness, bias, and the future of corporate accountability in the digital age. As the platform evolves, its terms of service will continue to play a crucial role in shaping the relationship between users, the platform, and the broader social media ecosystem.

CHAPTER EIGHT

A Changing Social Media Landscape: From Twitter to X

The transition of Twitter to X under Elon Musk's ownership has sparked a fundamental shift in the social media landscape. The changes have impacted everything from the platform's policies and user engagement to the broader industry's view on the role of social media in public discourse.

As X evolves, it is no longer just a rebranding exercise but a full-scale rethinking of what a social platform can be and how it can serve its users, advertisers, and political interests. This chapter explores the transformation of Twitter into X, the rise of alternative platforms, and the future of social media for high-profile figures like celebrities and journalists.

How Twitter's Identity Evolved Under Musk's Leadership

When Elon Musk acquired Twitter in 2022, he promised sweeping changes that would dramatically reshape the platform. Musk's vision for the platform revolved around making it a "town square" for free speech, where open discussion could take place without the constraints of content moderation and censorship. He argued that Twitter should foster an environment where all viewpoints, even controversial ones, could be expressed without restriction. This vision quickly became evident as Musk made significant changes to the platform's rules, staff, and features.

Under Musk's leadership, Twitter began to loosen its content moderation policies, which had previously been stricter under its previous management. One of the most high-profile changes was the reinstatement of accounts previously banned for violating the platform's rules on hate speech, misinformation, and incitement of violence.

This included the return of controversial figures such as former President Donald Trump, who had been banned for his role in the January 6th Capitol riot. The lifting of these bans was part of Musk's broader effort to restore what he considered the fundamental principles of free speech, albeit with critics warning that this could lead to a rise in harmful content.

Musk also introduced the concept of "X" as a replacement for the Twitter brand. The rebranding was initially seen as a bold move to usher in a new era for the platform, one that would go beyond social networking and expand into areas such as financial services, e-commerce, and more. Musk's vision for X was to create a "super app," similar to China's WeChat, that could integrate social media with other services such as payments, news, and entertainment, effectively making it a one-stop digital hub.

This shift to X also involved a reorganization of the platform's user interface and functionality. Musk introduced a subscription-based model called Twitter Blue, which allowed users to purchase verification badges and access premium features, such as longer tweets, additional customization options, and improved visibility. While these changes were designed to generate revenue for the platform and allow for greater user personalization, they also contributed to a growing sense of inequality on the platform, as paying users were given more privileges than non-paying ones.

However, despite Musk's lofty ambitions, X's evolution has been marked by significant controversy. As more users, including high-profile personalities and news organizations, began to leave the platform, concerns grew about the effectiveness of

Musk's vision. Critics argue that by prioritizing free speech over content moderation, X has allowed hate speech, disinformation, and extremist ideologies to flourish. Meanwhile, the platform's transformation has alienated some of its most dedicated users, who have criticized Musk for turning a once vibrant social media platform into a space filled with polarization and misinformation.

The Rise of Alternative Social Media Platforms

As X continues to evolve under Musk's leadership, other social media platforms have begun to capitalize on the shifting landscape, positioning themselves as viable alternatives for users seeking a more moderate or balanced experience. Platforms like Mastodon, Threads, and Bluesky have emerged as potential competitors to X, offering users an alternative to the freewheeling, often contentious environment of Musk's version of Twitter.

Mastodon, an open-source decentralized platform, gained significant traction in 2023 as users, particularly those disillusioned with Musk's changes, sought a more community-driven platform where content moderation was handled by individual servers rather than a central authority. Mastodon's emphasis on user autonomy and its lack of central control has made it an appealing alternative for those who want to avoid the issues that have plagued X, such as excessive commercialization, content moderation controversy, and rising toxicity.

Threads, launched by Meta in response to Musk's purchase of Twitter, quickly gained millions of users when it debuted in 2023. Unlike X, Threads focuses on fostering a more positive and community-driven environment, offering a feed for short posts and a more streamlined, user-friendly design. Meta's deep integration with Instagram has also made it easier for users to migrate from the photo-sharing platform to Threads, creating a more seamless transition for people seeking an alternative to X.

Bluesky, a social network backed by former Twitter CEO Jack Dorsey, offers a decentralized approach to social media, similar to Mastodon, but with a focus on maintaining privacy and transparency.

Bluesky seeks to combine the best of both worlds: the decentralized nature of Mastodon with a user experience closer to the traditional social media model. The platform has attracted a dedicated following from users disillusioned by X's policies, as well as privacy advocates who are concerned about Musk's data practices.

These emerging platforms have tapped into a growing frustration with X, providing users with more options for engagement and self-expression. They represent a shift away from the centralized power structures that have traditionally dominated social media, signaling a potential shift in how digital communication will evolve in the years to come. As these platforms grow, they may challenge Musk's vision for X, providing more diverse and potentially less divisive alternatives.

The Future of Social Media Engagement for Celebrities and Journalists

For celebrities and journalists, social media platforms like X have long been essential tools for building audiences, engaging with fans, and disseminating information. However, as the dynamics of social media continue to evolve, both groups face new challenges when it comes to navigating platforms that are increasingly politicized, commercially driven, and hostile to certain types of discourse.

The departure of high-profile figures such as Jamie Lee Curtis, Don Lemon, and The

Guardian illustrates a growing trend of celebrities and journalists distancing themselves from platforms like X. For many, the platform's shift in policies under Musk's leadership has made it harder to maintain professional integrity and engage in meaningful discussions. Public figures are increasingly concerned about the reputational risks associated with being part of a platform where misinformation, hate speech, and extremism are allowed to thrive.

Journalists, in particular, are facing increased pressure to balance their roles as objective reporters with the demands of platform algorithms that prioritize sensationalism over factual reporting. The rise of "news deserts," where quality journalism is being replaced by viral content and opinion-driven posts, has made it harder for journalists to maintain credibility in the digital age. As Musk's policies continue to prioritize engagement over quality, many journalists are questioning the value of using X to promote their work, particularly when the platform becomes a breeding ground for conspiracy theories, online harassment, and hate speech.

For celebrities, the shifting environment on platforms like X raises concerns about brand image and the potential risks of alienating fans. As social media becomes more polarized, celebrities must weigh the benefits of using these platforms to engage with their audiences against the risks of being associated with controversial content and toxic discourse. The increasing focus on profit-driven algorithms that reward outrage and sensationalism has created an environment that is often at odds with the personal and professional values of public figures.

Looking ahead, the future of social media engagement for both celebrities and journalists may involve a shift toward more curated, niche platforms that align with their personal and professional values. Platforms like Mastodon, Bluesky, and Threads could offer alternatives that provide a more moderated environment and greater control over content. Additionally, the growing trend toward decentralization may empower users—whether they are celebrities, journalists, or everyday people—to reclaim ownership of their online identities and interactions.

As the social media landscape continues to evolve, public figures may increasingly move toward platforms that align with their values, creating new opportunities for engagement that emphasize responsible content sharing, quality discourse, and greater accountability. Social media may no longer be a one-size-fits-all tool for engagement but a more fragmented ecosystem where individuals and organizations can select platforms that best serve their needs and align with their principles.

Overall, this chapter delves into the transformation of Twitter into X, examining how Musk's leadership has reshaped the platform and the social media landscape as a whole. It also explores the emergence of alternative platforms, such as Mastodon, Threads, and Bluesky, and the implications these shifts have for public figures like celebrities and journalists.

As social media continues to evolve, the future of online engagement will depend on how users, creators, and platforms navigate the changing dynamics of content, culture, and accountability in the digital age.

CHAPTER NINE

Celebrity and Media Integrity in the Digital Age

In the digital age, social media has become an essential tool for celebrities and media outlets, offering direct access to audiences and a platform to shape public personas, engage with fans, and promote their work. However, the dynamics of digital communication present unique ethical challenges, particularly as the platforms on which these figures interact with the public continue to evolve.

For many, maintaining integrity in the face of social media's vast reach and the political polarization of modern discourse has become increasingly difficult. This chapter explores the ethical considerations surrounding the social media use of public figures, the responsibility of platforms to uphold standards, and how these individuals navigate the complex and often contentious landscape of political polarization.

The Ethics of Public Figures' Social Media Use

For celebrities and journalists, social media represents both an opportunity and a responsibility. The instantaneous nature of platforms like X means that public figures can instantly connect with millions of people worldwide, but it also places them under the constant scrutiny of their followers and critics. The ethical implications of this level of visibility are multifaceted and often complex.

At the core of the ethical concerns surrounding public figures' use of social media is the issue of authenticity. Celebrities and journalists often use platforms like X to engage directly with their audiences, offering glimpses into their personal lives, thoughts, and opinions.

However, the curated nature of social media means that much of what is shared is selective, leading to a tension between the public persona and the private individual. As followers increasingly demand more transparency, public figures may struggle with the ethics of oversharing or misrepresenting themselves online, which can have consequences for their professional and personal lives.

Furthermore, the ethics of influence is a key consideration. Celebrities and journalists hold a significant amount of sway over their audiences, and with that power comes the responsibility to be mindful of the messages they promote. Whether endorsing products, political views, or social movements, public figures are expected to wield their influence in ways that align with ethical standards.

This becomes particularly tricky in an age of corporate sponsorships, where celebrities may be paid to promote certain narratives or products, creating potential conflicts of interest. The ethical issue arises when the lines between personal belief and commercial interest blur, especially when the public figure's stance on controversial issues may be seen as financially motivated or misleading.

Lastly, celebrities and journalists must consider the potential impact of their online actions on vulnerable audiences. Given the influence they wield, public figures are expected to adhere to certain standards of conduct that prevent them from spreading misinformation, inciting hatred, or reinforcing harmful stereotypes.

Their posts can have real-world consequences, particularly when it comes to topics like mental health, race, and social justice. For example, a celebrity endorsing or dismissing certain medical treatments can shape public opinion, affecting how their followers approach health-related issues. Similarly, a journalist's choice to amplify or disregard a particular political narrative can have lasting effects on the public's understanding of critical issues.

As the ethics of social media engagement continue to evolve, celebrities and journalists must navigate these challenges thoughtfully. Striking a balance between personal expression, professional responsibility, and public influence is a complex task that requires an ongoing commitment to authenticity and accountability.

The Responsibility of Platforms to Uphold Standards

While public figures are expected to adhere to ethical standards, the platforms on which they operate must also play a critical role in ensuring that these standards are upheld. The responsibility of social media companies to foster a healthy, ethical environment has come under increasing scrutiny, especially as platforms become more influential in shaping public discourse and political outcomes.

In the past, platforms like Twitter (now X) have claimed to operate as neutral spaces for free speech, allowing users to share their opinions without interference. However, as the volume of harmful content, such as disinformation, hate speech, and harassment, has grown, the question of platform responsibility has become central to the conversation around social media ethics.

Social media platforms have faced increasing pressure from both users and governments to regulate harmful content, with some arguing that platforms have a duty to protect users from toxic or misleading content, while others insist that platforms should remain neutral and not interfere in users' right to free speech.

Under Elon Musk's leadership, X has loosened its content moderation policies, removing certain safeguards that were previously in place to curb harmful speech. This has led to accusations that the platform is enabling the spread of hate speech, conspiracy theories, and extremist rhetoric. Critics argue that by prioritizing free speech and reducing content moderation, Musk's X has become a less safe environment for users, particularly marginalized groups who are more vulnerable to online abuse. In contrast, advocates for less regulation argue that content moderation stifles free expression and that users should be responsible for managing what they see online.

In light of these debates, platforms are increasingly being called upon to implement clearer, more consistent standards for content moderation, one that balances free speech with the need to protect users from harm. This includes enforcing rules against hate speech, misinformation, and harassment while also ensuring that users are not silenced for expressing legitimate opinions.

For public figures, the platform's stance on these issues is critical because it dictates the kind of environment in which they engage with their audiences. A platform that lacks robust moderation practices risks enabling harmful rhetoric that can undermine public discourse and tarnish the reputations of those who choose to participate in it.

Moreover, social media platforms are increasingly facing government and legal pressure to comply with laws aimed at curbing harmful content. In Europe, the Digital Services Act (DSA) mandates that platforms like X take greater responsibility for removing illegal content and protecting users from harmful practices.

Similarly, in the United States, lawmakers are debating proposals to regulate tech companies more tightly, particularly in the areas of privacy, transparency, and accountability. These evolving legal frameworks present platforms with the challenge of balancing business interests with public safety and ethics.

The responsibility of platforms to uphold standards goes beyond merely enforcing rules—it involves fostering a culture that encourages ethical behavior from both users and companies. To maintain the trust of users, celebrities, journalists, and advertisers, platforms must demonstrate a commitment to fairness, transparency, and the protection of public safety.

Navigating Political Polarization in Public Communication

In today's polarized political environment, navigating social media as a public figure is an increasingly fraught endeavor. Social media platforms have become battlegrounds for political ideologies, and public figures often find themselves caught in the crossfire. The rise of hyper-partisan discourse and the spread of political misinformation on platforms like X have made it harder for celebrities and journalists to maintain neutral ground without being drawn into the divisive conversations that dominate the space.

For celebrities and journalists, navigating political polarization requires an awareness of the risks associated with taking stances on controversial issues. Public figures who express political opinions often face backlash from opposing factions, leading to a loss of followers, brand deals, or professional opportunities. However, the pressure to remain silent or avoid taking positions can also lead to accusations of inauthenticity or complicity, particularly in the age of cancel culture, where people expect public figures to take clear stances on important issues.

The political polarization on social media also affects how public figures engage with their audiences. In many cases, celebrities and journalists are forced to choose between appeasing their followers or maintaining their ethical integrity.

Celebrities, for example, may risk alienating fans who disagree with their political views, while journalists may face pressure to cater to certain political narratives, even at the expense of their journalistic objectivity. As social media platforms increasingly become sites for political battles, the ethical challenge for public figures is to strike a balance between expressing their beliefs and maintaining a respectful, open environment for dialogue.

Moreover, the spread of disinformation on platforms like X has further complicated the ability of public figures to communicate with their audiences in a trustworthy way.

Political groups and bad actors often weaponize social media to spread misleading narratives or attack opposing figures, creating an environment where every post or tweet can be taken out of context or misrepresented. In this polarized environment, public figures must carefully consider the impact of their words, as their statements may be amplified or distorted in ways that can undermine public trust and personal credibility.

To navigate these challenges, public figures must develop a strategy for engaging with political content that aligns with their values while also being mindful of the broader consequences of their actions. This includes understanding the risks of participating in divisive debates, taking a stand on important issues, and, when necessary, choosing to disengage from harmful or toxic conversations.

Overall, this chapter explores the ethical considerations surrounding the use of social media by public figures, the role of platforms in upholding standards, and the challenges posed by political polarization. As social media continues to shape public discourse, the responsibility of both public figures and platforms in maintaining integrity has never been more critical.

Celebrities and journalists must navigate a complex landscape that requires them to balance personal beliefs, professional responsibilities, and public expectations while also ensuring that their engagement on digital platforms promotes healthy, constructive dialogue.

CHAPTER TEN

The Aftermath of Departures: The Future of X and Its Users

The departure of prominent figures like Jamie Lee Curtis, Don Lemon, and major media outlets such as The Guardian has left a significant mark on X (formerly Twitter), reshaping its reputation and casting doubt on the platform's future. These exits, driven by political, ethical, and legal concerns, serve as a reflection of the broader issues facing social media platforms in a rapidly changing digital and political landscape.

As users, brands, and celebrities reconsider their relationship with X, the platform is forced to reckon with the consequences of these high-profile departures. In this chapter, we examine the immediate aftermath of these exits, explore the potential for X's recovery, and consider what the future holds for social media platforms and their diverse users.

The Impact of High-Profile Departures on X's Reputation

The exits of Jamie Lee Curtis, Don Lemon, and The Guardian are more than just departures from a single platform—they signal a broader crisis of credibility and trust for X. These high-profile individuals and institutions were not merely passive users but influential figures whose presence lent legitimacy and vibrancy to the platform. Their departure reflects growing concerns about the platform's direction under Elon Musk's leadership, particularly its increasing embrace of controversial political figures and content moderation changes.

Public figures and media outlets leaving X is not just a loss of content creators but also a blow to the platform's reputation as a space for diverse voices and healthy discourse. Celebrities like Curtis, who were once enthusiastic users, help draw in everyday users, and their departure weakens the community's sense of inclusion and connection. Lemon's legal disputes with X, along with his high-profile statement on the state of the platform, underscore deeper concerns about transparency and the platform's dedication to upholding free speech in a fair and balanced manner.

The media's retreat from X, as seen with The Guardian, underscores the sense of growing toxicity around the platform, which has been linked to the spread of disinformation, harassment, and far-right rhetoric. These departures also have ripple effects, as other influencers, celebrities, and organizations may follow suit. When these respected entities exit, it's often seen as a signal to other users that the platform is no longer a viable space for professional, objective discourse.

This shift poses a challenge for Musk's vision of X as a platform that can embrace free speech without censorship. With the loss of some of its most respected users, the platform risks further alienating mainstream audiences.

Additionally, the departure of these influential figures raises questions about X's marketability. Brands and advertisers closely monitor the activity and trustworthiness of social platforms, and the departure of trusted public figures may deter them from continuing or starting campaigns on the platform. The perception that X is no longer a safe, credible place for discussion could lead to a decline in advertising revenue and user engagement, further hurting its long-term viability.

Could X Recover Its Credibility?

The question of whether X can recover from the aftermath of these high-profile departures depends on several factors: its leadership decisions, its approach to content moderation, and its ability to address the concerns that have caused many of its users to leave. Musk's vision for X, which has included reducing content moderation, emphasizing free speech, and restructuring the platform, has proven to be controversial.

Many argue that Musk's laissez-faire approach has opened the door for the spread of toxic content, conspiracy theories, and hate speech, all of which contribute to an environment that is increasingly hostile to certain communities and perspectives.

For X to recover its credibility, Musk will need to demonstrate a clear commitment to addressing the issues that have driven users away. This could include reinstating more robust content moderation practices, enforcing stricter rules against harmful speech, and creating a safer space for users of all political leanings. Furthermore, X could invest in increasing transparency around its policies and decisions, particularly when it comes to how content is promoted or suppressed on the platform.

Rebuilding trust is a slow process that requires consistency and accountability. Musk must also demonstrate that X is a platform that values its user base, including marginalized communities, journalists, and public figures, who rely on social media for engagement and professional growth. A significant part of this recovery process will be showing that X is a responsible platform where important social issues can be discussed respectfully and inclusively.

Another challenge for X's recovery lies in its competition with other platforms. As many users leave X, they are increasingly turning to alternative platforms that offer similar social media experiences without the same level of controversy. Platforms like Mastodon, Threads, and BlueSky are emerging as alternatives for users who feel disenfranchised by X's current direction. If these competitors can offer a more supportive, inclusive, and safe environment, X's ability to regain user loyalty will be even more difficult.

Ultimately, X's recovery will depend on Musk's ability to adjust his approach and make meaningful changes that address the concerns voiced by high-profile users and media outlets. If the platform continues to be seen as a venue for political polarization and misinformation, it is unlikely to recover its former position as a trusted social media space.

What's Next for Celebrities, Journalists, and Social Media Platforms

As X faces a potential decline in trust and user engagement, the future of social media platforms and their role in the lives of celebrities, journalists, and the general public is at a crossroads. Celebrities and journalists, who have long relied on social media to reach their audiences and shape their public personas, are now reassessing their options. For some, the alternatives to X may present more opportunities for authentic engagement without the ethical and political concerns that dominate the platform.

For celebrities and influencers, platforms like Instagram, YouTube, and TikTok continue to offer avenues for personal branding and professional growth. These platforms have a more controlled environment, where content creators can maintain a consistent image and connect with followers in meaningful ways. However, the departure from X signals that celebrities may be seeking platforms that provide more than just a space for content creation—they are looking for platforms that prioritize safety, inclusivity, and transparency.

Journalists, similarly, may look to diversify their digital engagement by turning to platforms with stronger editorial guidelines or establishing their own channels of communication. Given the growing concerns over media bias and misinformation on platforms like X, more journalists might choose to take their work to independent platforms or subscription-based services where they can cultivate a more controlled audience and protect their journalistic integrity.

In fact, many media outlets, such as The Guardian, have already begun to move away from X, reassessing the value of maintaining a presence on the platform versus focusing on other forms of outreach to their audiences.

The evolving landscape of social media also means that we may see new platforms rise to prominence. The growing dissatisfaction with platforms like X has created room for the development of alternative social media services, such as Mastodon, which prioritize decentralized governance and stronger moderation practices.

These platforms are particularly attractive to users who are disillusioned by the political and ethical challenges of current giants like X and Facebook. Whether these platforms can compete with the established players remains to be seen, but they represent a potential shift in the way social media operates in the coming years.

As for X, its future will largely depend on its ability to adapt to the changing needs of its users and the broader social media ecosystem. If it continues to cater primarily to a conservative base while neglecting the concerns of the broader public, it risks becoming a niche platform. However, if X embraces a more balanced, transparent approach to content moderation and user engagement, it may find a way to regain its position as a leading social media platform.

In conclusion, the aftershocks of high-profile departures from X are just the beginning of a larger shift in the social media landscape. As celebrities, journalists, and users navigate an increasingly polarized digital world, the platforms that succeed will be those that prioritize ethical standards, protect free speech, and maintain trust with their communities. Whether X can recover its credibility remains uncertain, but the lessons learned from these departures will undoubtedly influence the future of social media.

CONCLUSION

The departure of influential figures from X marks a pivotal moment in the evolution of social media, revealing underlying tensions between the platform's leadership and its user base. High-profile exits by individuals such as Jamie Lee Curtis, Don Lemon, and major media outlets like The Guardian underscore deeper concerns about the direction of X under Elon Musk's ownership.

As the platform transitions from Twitter to X, the growing political polarization, legal battles, and shifting content policies have raised serious questions about its ability to maintain its status as a reliable space for free speech, responsible journalism, and online engagement.

The controversies surrounding X are emblematic of broader shifts occurring within social media ecosystems globally. Musk's emphasis on free speech, often without adequate content moderation, has fueled an environment ripe for misinformation, harassment, and political extremism.

The consequences of these changes have not only eroded trust among public figures and the media but also impacted how ordinary users perceive the platform. For many, the promise of X as a space for open, transparent dialogue has been overshadowed by concerns about censorship, legal biases, and the increasing dominance of far-right narratives.

The legal and political influences that have shaped the platform's transformation cannot be ignored. Musk's involvement in political discourse, particularly his close ties to figures like former President Donald Trump, has created a charged atmosphere on X. As the platform's policies and political affiliations become more pronounced, it risks alienating a significant portion of its user base who feel that the platform no longer serves its original purpose of fostering civil debate.

The legal shift to Texas courts, combined with Musk's increasing political influence, further complicates the platform's future, as it may discourage users who are wary of legal biases and the consolidation of power within a select few.

However, the exits of celebrities and journalists from X also point to a larger shift in the digital age: the evolving role of social media in public communication. As social media platforms become more integrated into the daily lives of people worldwide, their influence extends beyond just social interaction—they now play a critical role in shaping political discourse, public opinion, and media consumption. This reality brings with it both opportunities and challenges, as platforms face increasing pressure to balance free expression with the need to protect users from harmful content and ensure a fair, transparent environment.

The rise of alternative social media platforms like Mastodon, BlueSky, and Threads signals a potential shift toward more decentralized, community-driven online spaces. These platforms, which prioritize user control and content moderation, may offer a more attractive alternative for individuals and organizations looking for a more balanced and ethical online environment.

While these platforms are still in their infancy and have yet to challenge the dominance of giants like X, their growing popularity reflects a desire for more accountable social media spaces—spaces that respect privacy, uphold journalistic integrity, and provide a safer, more inclusive space for dialogue.

In the wake of these high-profile departures, X faces a critical juncture in its existence. Can the platform adapt to the changing demands of its users, rebuild trust, and recover from its current reputation? Or will it continue down a path of increasing polarization and legal entanglements? The platform's future hinges on its ability to find a balance between fostering free expression and ensuring that its environment is one that values ethical standards, protects vulnerable users, and promotes civil discourse.

As we move forward in the digital age, it's clear that the relationship between social media platforms and their users will continue to evolve. The growing awareness of the ethical, political, and legal implications of social media use has created a more discerning, vocal user base that demands more from the platforms they use. Celebrities, journalists, and ordinary citizens alike are no longer passive consumers of content but active participants in shaping the platforms that host their discourse.

The journey of X, from its rise as Twitter to its transformation under Musk's leadership, reflects the broader challenges and opportunities facing social media in today's world. It is a reminder that platforms are not static entities—they are shaped by the choices of their users, their leadership, and the political and legal forces that influence them.

As social media continues to be a dominant force in modern communication, the lessons from X's transformation will serve as a cautionary tale and a guide for how future platforms might navigate the complex interplay between free speech, regulation, and user trust.

In conclusion, the mass exodus from X underscores a significant shift in how celebrities, journalists, and everyday users view the platform and its future. While the platform's transformation is ongoing, it also reflects broader trends in social media's role in society and the ethical questions that arise from its immense influence. The departure of trusted voices calls attention to the crucial need for social media platforms to reassess their commitment to maintaining a space for responsible discourse, transparency, and ethical engagement.

The future of social media platforms will depend on their ability to adapt to these changing demands and rebuild trust with their diverse, global audiences. As we look toward the future, the challenge remains: can X—and social media in general—evolve into a space that truly serves the needs of its users while upholding the principles of free expression and accountability?

Printed in the USA
CPSIA information can be obtained
at www.ICGtesting.com
CBHW062024291124
18176CB00048B/884